Fox, Beware!

Written by **Judy Waite**
Illustrated by **Myriam Deru**

Rigby®
A Harcourt Achieve Imprint

www.Rigby.com
1-800-531-5015

Once there were days when
the woods were peaceful.
The fox snuggled safely
in her secret lair.
But now on the breeze
comes the scent of danger.
Something is coming.
Fox, beware!

**A man with a rope
is measuring and
muttering.**

Hurry now, fox.
You can't stay there!

3

There are soft-colored days
when the birds are nesting.
The fox lies still in a new-found lair.
But out of the quiet
grows a grumbling rumble.
Something is coming.
Fox, beware!

**The razor-toothed diggers
are ripping and wrecking.**

Hurry now, fox.

You can't stay there!

There are blazing days
in the burst of summer.
The fox stays cool
in a deep dark lair.
But the beautiful trees
are troubled and trembling.
Something is coming.
Fox, beware!

**The woodcutters' saws
are screeching and tearing.**

Hurry now, fox.

You can't stay there!

There are leaf-crackling days
when the trees turn golden.
The fox keeps watch
from a riverbank lair.
But with the hard rain
comes seeping and creeping.
Something is coming.
Fox, beware!

**The swollen brown river
is rushing and rising.**
Hurry now, fox.
You can't stay there!

There are bleak, bitter days
in the blast of winter.
The fox is cold
in her ice-fringed lair.
But down the old track
comes a digging and drilling.
Something is coming.
Fox, beware!

Cars race and roar
on the slick new surface.

Hurry now, fox.

You can't stay there!

11

Now the wild wood
has a hundred houses.
Hurrying people are everywhere.

And down by the fence
the fox still searches,
scrabbling and scratching
a safe new lair . . .

. . . while out of their window
the children are watching . . .

Relax now, fox.

You'll be safe there.